THEY DIED TOO YOUNG

BRUCE LEE

Jon E. Lewis

CHELSEA HOUSE PUBLISHERS
Philadelphia

First published in traditional hardback edition
© 1998 by Chelsea House Publishers,
a subsidiary of Haights Cross Communications
Printed in Malaysia
Copyright © Parragon Book Service Ltd 1995
Unit 13–17, Avonbridge Trading Estate, Atlantic Road
Avonmouth, Bristol, England BS11 9QD

Library of Congress Cataloging-in-Publication Data
Lewis, Jon E., 1961-
    Bruce Lee / by Jon E. Lewis.
        p.   cm. — (They died too young)
    Filmography: p.
    Summary: Chronicles the career and early death of the kung fu
    instructor who became a world-wide legend as the star of some of
    the greatest martial arts movies ever made.
    ISBN 0-7910-4635-4 (hardcover)
        1. Lee, Bruce, 1940-1973 — Juvenile literature. 2. Actors—United
    States--Biography—Juvenile literature. 3. Martial artists—United
    States--Biography—Juvenile literature. [1. Lee, Bruce,
    1940-1973. 2. Actors and actresses. 3. Martial artists.]
    I. Title. II. Series.
    PN2287.L2897L48   1997
    791.43'028'092—dc21
        [B]   97-15064
                                                                              CIP
                                                                              AC

Illustrations courtesy of Aquarius; Kobal Collection;
Concord/Warner Brothers (courtesy Kobal);
Golden Harvest (courtesy Kobal);
National General Pictures (courtesy Kobal)

CONTENTS

The young Bruce Lee

ENTER THE DRAGON

Long, long ago in medieval China, a wandering Buddhist monk by the name of Bodhidharma arrived at the Shaolin Cha'n Temple in the remote Songshan Mountains. He found the sacred temple almost in ruins and its monks stricken with starvation and disease. To improve their health, Bodhidharma developed a system of exercises based on yoga. He called the system the Eighteen Hands of Lo-Han. Over time the system of Eighteen Hands evolved into temple boxing, and thence into a martial art known as kung fu. In the 1700s the monks began to teach their methods to outsiders, and gradually knowledge of kung fu spread throughout China. Yet it might have remained within the borders of that ancient and mystical land if not for a young Hong Kong Chinese, Lee Jun Fan, who became a worldwide legend as the star of the greatest martial arts movies ever made.

Only his family knew him as Lee Jun Fan, though. Everybody else knew him as Bruce Lee.

Bruce Lee was born in the Year of the Dragon, on November 27, 1940. The city of his birth was San Francisco, but this was largely accidental. His father, Lee Hoi Chuen, was a minor star of the Cantonese Opera Company of Hong Kong, and at the time was touring the United States with a production called *The Drunken Princess*.

Lee Hoi and his wife, Grace—who already had one son and two daughters—named their newest offspring Lee Jun Fan, which means "Return again." A strong intuition told them that this son would one day come back to America to live. A nurse at the Jackson Street Hospital in Chinatown suggested an English-language first name, Bruce, for his American birth certificate. Most of the time the family referred to the new baby as Sai Fong ("Small Phoenix"), a girl's name. Like many Chinese, Lee Hoi and Grace were deeply superstitious. A previous son had died, so by calling Bruce by a girl's name they believed the spirits would be confused, and therefore unable to steal away his soul. The Lees also quickly gave Bruce the nickname Mo si tung ("Never sits still"). Even from earliest infancy, Bruce was possessed by a remarkable, restless energy.

Early in 1941, the Lee family returned home to the British Crown Colony of Hong Kong, the most densely populated city on earth. They rented a thirteenth-floor two-bedroom apartment at 218 Nathan Road, Kowloon. Squeezed into its small square footage was the Lee family (later joined by another son, Robert) and Lee Hoi Chuen's sister-in-law and her five children—some twenty people in all, including servants.

The Lees, like other Hong Kong citizens, had other problems besides overcrowding. Bruce's early years were overshadowed by the Japanese occupation of 1942–45, a long nightmare of starvation and brutality. One of Bruce's earliest memories was standing on the roof of No. 218 shaking his fist at a Japanese plane flying low overhead.

With the eventual departure of the Japanese in 1945, driven out by the terror of day-and-night Allied bombing, the people of the city began the slow task of reconstruction, not just of roads and buildings, but of lives and livelihoods. Among the first industries to be revived was the entertainment business, and Lee Hoi Chuen soon found himself back in regular acting work.

Through his father's show business connections, Bruce Lee became a child movie star. At the age of six, after frequently accompanying his father to film shoots, Bruce was given a role in the Hong Kong film *The Beginning of a Boy*. (Although Bruce considered this his official film debut, it was not his first appearance on screen: at the age of three months he had been carried in front of the camera for a part in a Chinese film shot in San Francisco.) Two years after *The Beginning of a Boy* he played his second role, under the stage name Lee Siu Lung ("Lee Little Dragon")—the name by which he would become famous in Hong Kong and on the burgeoning Mandarin film circuit, and which would explain the title of some of his later, adult pictures. By the time Bruce Lee was eighteen, he had appeared in twenty films, including *The Orphan*, a 1958 Hong Kong teen classic in which he took the lead role as juvenile delinquent.

Bruce Lee was well cast. Outside of the studio walls he was exactly the sort of gang boy he played in *The Orphan*. As he told *Black Belt* magazine in 1967, "I was a punk [as a teenager] and went looking for fights." He had not done well at school. As his mother recollected later, only half jokingly, "By the age of ten, that was as far as he could count." After Chinese primary school, he had entered La Salle College, an English-speaking Catholic institution where he proved uninterested and inattentive and his grades were mediocre. He was expelled for disruptive behavior. His parents enrolled him at another Hong Kong Catholic college, St. Francis Xavier, but there was no improvement. Bruce Lee, despite his bookish glasses, was not the scholastic type.

So, like other Hong Kong Chinese kids, he turned to the streets to find his identity. He explained later, "Kids in Hong Kong have nothing to look forward to. The [British] have all the best jobs and the rest of us had to work for them. That's why most of the kids become punks. . . . Kids in slums can never get out." As a gang boy his principal activity was street fighting. Sometimes he armed himself with a chain; more often he just used his fists and his feet, which were already formidable weapons.

Bruce Lee began learning kung fu in 1949, the same year that Mao Tse-tung's Red Army swept across mainland China, only to halt at the very gates of Hong Kong, frightened by the threat of a confrontation with the city's imperial British overseer. Oblivious to this grand drama, nine-year-old Bruce Lee had run home from school one day and complained to his parents of being bullied. He said he wanted to be trained in the martial arts. His father practiced *tai chi*, but Bruce found this too slow for his taste, so his parents agreed to pay for him to receive lessons from Sifu Yip Man, a great master of the *wing chun* ("beautiful springtime") school of kung fu.

Yip Man had been born in the town of Fatshan, but had left before the Communist takeover, settling in Hong Kong. There, not far from Tang City Hall, he had founded his *kwoon* (training club) in an abandoned back-street temple. For ten years, from 1949 through 1959, Bruce Lee attended Yip Man's *kwoon* to learn the secrets of *wing chun*, constantly growing in *chi* (inner energy) and skill. As a style, *wing chun* suited the slightly built Bruce well. Developed by a Chinese village woman under the tutelage of a Shaolin nun, *wing chun* was fluid and economical, turning the opponent's force against him or her.

Bruce Lee's devotion to kung fu was total. At home, during dinner, he pounded away on a stool with alternate hands to toughen them. Through Yip Man, he also became interested in the philosophical teachings of Confucius, Buddha, Lao-Tze, and the other influential thinkers of the East.

By the age of eighteen, Bruce Lee was a kung fu adept and had begun to form his own ideas of style. In particular, his experience of street fighting had shown him the limitations of *wing chun*. On the mean streets of Hong Kong, the world's busiest city, assailants did not bow respectfully before fighting or follow ancient and fair rules. They attacked with surprise and lethal weapons. The key to a modern,

They Died Too Young

successful martial art, Bruce Lee believed, was adaptability. Yet he retained a respectful loyalty to Yip Man and *wing chun*, and it was this loyalty that eventually obliged him to leave Hong Kong. In early 1959 a challenge was issued to the students of the Wing Chun School by the pupils of a rival establishment, the Choi Li Fut School. The two groups met on the roof of an apartment block in the Resettlement Area. What was meant to be a nonviolent sparring encounter soon turned ugly. When an opponent gave Bruce a black eye, Bruce responded with an angry series of straight punches and high kicks, catching his opponent in the eye and mouth and knocking out a tooth. The boy's parents complained to the police and Bruce was arrested. To secure his release, Mrs. Lee was obliged to sign a paper assuming responsibility for Bruce's future conduct.

A family council agreed that it would be wise to send Bruce away, out of trouble's way—to America. And so Bruce Lee, as his Chinese name had predicted, returned to San Francisco, the city of his birth.

Bruce Lee

AMERICA

The American President Lines steamship took eighteen days to make the journey from Hong Kong to San Francisco. Bruce spent the crossing teaching cha-cha dancing to the passengers in first class (he had been the Hong Kong cha-cha champion the previous year). He also rid himself of the last vestiges of Lee Jun Fan, and he carefully practiced his English on his fellow passengers.

He landed in America as Bruce Lee, U.S. citizen, with a mere $100 to his new name. At first he lived in Chinatown and earned a little money giving dance classes. Then Ruby Chow, a Seattle restaurant owner who was a friend of his father's, offered Bruce a room in return for his evening services as a waiter.

The chance of a steady job was simply too good to miss. Arriving in Seattle, Bruce enrolled as a day student at the Edison Technical School—his rebellious boyhood had been dumped overboard from the trans-Pacific liner along with the rest of Lee Jun Fan—and quickly earned his high school diploma. This enabled him to be admitted to the University of Washington, enrolling in the autumn of 1962 to study philosophy.

It was in Seattle that Bruce started teaching kung fu (although he preferred the pronunciation "gung fu"), at first to small groups of Asian martial arts fans, and later to anybody of any race who happened to be interested. As he taught, Bruce constantly worked on progressing his own universal, simplified, fluid version of kung fu, which he would later term *jeet kune do* ("the way of intercepting fist"). "To me 99 percent of the whole business of Oriental self-defense is baloney," he once stated. "It's fancy jazz. It looks good but it doesn't work." Inevitably, Bruce's opinion on the classic martial arts caused offense to their practitioners. A Japanese karate black belt attending one of Bruce's demonstrations challenged him to a fight to determine who had the superior method. Using a series of straight *wing chun* punches followed by a Thai boxing-style kick to the face, Bruce won in seconds.

Though kung fu may have been an Eastern method of self-defense, Bruce soon realized that it could be used to achieve the American Dream—to make money. Late in 1963 he opened the Jun Fan Gung Fu Institute at 4750 University Way in Seattle, the first *kwoon* in what Bruce intended to be an America-wide chain. The regular fee was $22 per month.

Not all of Bruce's mind was concentrated on his philosophical studies, kung fu, and money, however. On October 26, 1963, he went on a date with Linda Emery, a fellow University of Washington student who sometimes attended his kung fu classes. Linda Emery was Caucasian, of English and Swedish descent. Realizing that her mother (her father had died when she was five) would object to her going out with an Asian, she arranged for Bruce to pick her up in his Ford '57 from a girlfriend's house. After what Linda later remembered as a "perfect evening," with dinner at the revolving restaurant at the top of the Seattle Space Needle, the couple continued to date regularly throughout the rest of 1963 and into the summer of 1964.

By June of 1964, Bruce had decided to give up his studies at the University of Washington and move to Oakland, California, where he intended to open a second

They Died Too Young

branch of the Jun Fan Gung Fu Institute, in partnership with his friend James Y. Lee. Linda Emery took him to the airport. Bruce promised to return, but she was not sure that he would.

After several months of ardent letter writing, Bruce—as good as his word—flew back to Seattle, where he asked Linda to marry him. She immediately agreed. To avoid the inevitable wrath of the Emery family, they decided not to inform them beforehand and instead to tell them afterward with the plan completed. But things went wrong almost immediately. Under a Seattle bylaw, those applying for a marriage license must wait a mandatory three days. Moreover—and unknown to Bruce and Linda—the names of the applicants are published in a local paper. And it was there that Linda's Aunt Sally saw Linda's name and that of a Bruce J. F. Lee, and read of their intent to marry.

Once alerted, the Emery family tried desperately to stop the interracial wedding. But the opposition of the Emerys only convinced Bruce and Linda that they were doing the right thing, and on August 17, 1964, they married. Days later they moved to Oakland. Bruce had already written to his family telling them of his plan to wed an American girl. The racial barrier was less of a problem to the Lees, for it had already been broken in their family: Bruce's mother, Grace, was half German.

The Oakland Gung Fu Institute soon had a full roster of students. But success sometimes attracts trouble as well as reward, as Bruce was to find out. In December 1964, when he was taking a class at the Institute, a message arrived from the elders of San Francisco's Chinatown. There was an unwritten Chinese law that the secrets of China's martial arts should not be taught to Westerners. The elders wanted Bruce to end the lessons to non-Asians. Bruce refused. Less than a week later, a kung fu practitioner arrived at Bruce's *kwoon*, accompanied by several elders. The expert gave Bruce an ornate scroll formally challenging him to a fight. If Bruce lost, he was either to close down the institute or stop teaching Caucasians.

A furious Bruce Lee accepted the challenge immediately. One minute later the expert was on the run before a fusillade of straight punches. The two men returned to the center of the gym, and Bruce quickly felled his opponent. With Bruce's fist poised above his face, the expert surrendered. Bruce was never again bothered by the Chinese elders.

Although Bruce had emerged victorious from the fight, he had not been satisfied with his performance and believed that he should have won more quickly. He was already fit and immensely strong for his weight (150 pounds) and height (a little over five-foot-seven), but he now sought physical perfection. In particular he concentrated on the muscular development of his torso and abdomen. To improve his punches and kicks—one of the weakest, most neglected aspects of Chinese martial arts—he practiced endlessly on a *wing chun* wooden dummy, a thick, six-foot-high cylinder from which protruded three "arms" and one "leg." But most of all, he sparred at every available opportunity with his students and other kung fu practitioners.

The year 1965 opened with both joy and pain for Bruce. A son, Brandon, was born in February. A week later, Bruce's father died. Meanwhile, the Oakland Gung Fu Institute, after its initial good start, was doing less well than had been hoped—not least because Bruce would only admit the most committed pupils. Bruce began to consider abandoning kung fu as a way of earning a living.

At the end of February, as Bruce pessimistically pondered his future, he received a phone call from a television producer named William Dozier. Dozier had seen some footage of Bruce in action at the 1964 Karate Internationals at Long Beach. He wanted Bruce for "Number One Son" in a television version of Charlie Chan. Would Bruce be interested? He was, and drove to Hollywood for a screen test. The reaction was positive.

By now, however, Dozier had decided to scrap the Charlie Chan idea. *Batman* was about to air on television and if it did well in the ratings, Dozier wanted to follow it up with a show based on another crime-fighting comic strip character, *The Green Hornet*. Bruce would play the part of Kato, the chauffeur and sidekick to hero Britt Reid. This would not happen for a year, but in the meantime Bruce was put under option for a fee of $1,800. Bruce later joked that he got the part because he was the only Chinese in the United States who could say "Britt Reid."

Bruce used the windfall to pay for a lengthy trip to Hong Kong, so his family could meet Linda and Brandon. They returned to the States late in the year, to be told the good news by Dozier that *The Green Hornet* was going ahead. With Hollywood beckoning, Bruce and Linda moved to Los Angeles in March 1966, taking a small apartment on Wilshire Boulevard in Westwood. The studio, Twentieth Century-Fox, also arranged for Bruce to receive acting lessons, the only "proper" instruction in the thespian art that he ever received.

Game of Death, *poised to leap*

THE GREEN HORNET

The Green Hornet went into production in 1966. At that time only one other Asian actor was featured in a network television show, Japanese-American George Takei, in the then-low-rated *Star Trek*. The network, wary of casting a Chinese actor as a costar in the days when there was little multiracial casting, insisted that in his role as Kato, Bruce wear a black mask over his face for most of his time on screen.

The Green Hornet lasted only six months. It lacked the camp humor of *Batman*, and adults found it corny. Everybody, though, from kids to critics, were dazzled by Bruce's kung fu. "He strikes with such speed that he makes a rattler look like a study in slow motion," wrote one pundit. The show made Bruce famous and he applied himself to cultivating his celebrity status. Dressed in his Kato uniform of jet-black chauffeur's suit and cap, plus mask, he made personal appearances, rode on floats at parades, and signed autographs. At karate demonstrations he gave vivid displays of his strength, including one-finger push-ups. Enthusiastic fans mobbed him in the street. It was his first taste of fame and he liked it.

The cancellation of *The Green Hornet* was a blow not just to Bruce's ego but to his wallet. He had been paid $400 a week during filming and drove a red Porsche. Now, suddenly, he was forced back to a dwindling income from the *kwoon*, plus an occasional guest spot in the television shows *Here Come the Brides, Longstreet, Blondie,* and *Ironside.* There was also a bit part in the 1969 movie *Marlowe,* starring James Garner; it was Bruce's first appearance in a Hollywood feature-length film. (The scene in which Bruce meets Marlowe on the roof of the Los Angeles Occidental Building and takes a screaming dive off the edge is one of the most memorable in the movie.) Additionally, he worked on a script for a martial arts film, *The Silent Flute,* which Warner Bros. expressed interest in and even sent Bruce to India to hunt locations, but eventually the studio turned it down. Later, when Bruce was long dead but extremely famous, and martial arts had become a Western craze, Warner Bros. would opportunistically film a version of the script, *Circle of Iron,* with David Carradine in the lead role.

At the suggestion of Charles Fitzsimon, the assistant producer on *The Green Hornet,* Bruce began giving private kung fu lessons—at $50 per hour—to Hollywood stars. Among Bruce's students were Steve McQueen and James Coburn (who became close personal friends), Elke Sommer, director Roman Polanski, and screenwriter Stirling Silliphant. Also receiving personal instruction from Bruce during this period were the karate experts Joe Lewis, Mike Stone, and Chuck Norris. Between them, Lewis, Stone, and Norris would go on to win every major karate championship in the United States.

Yet the Lee family finances remained perilous. A mortgage on a house in Los Angeles was a particular drain. To make matters worse, in 1970 Bruce injured himself badly during a weight-lifting session. The diagnosis was that he had permanently damaged his fourth sacral nerve. Not only would he need months of bed rest, the doctors informed him, but he would never practice kung fu again.

Depressed, barely able to move, and with the Porsche

about to be repossessed, Bruce—who had very traditional views on the roles of husbands and wives—consented to let Linda go out to work. She got a job as receptionist with an answering service. Bruce stayed at home looking after Brandon and the Lees' new arrival, daughter Shannon, born in 1969. He also undertook an extensive study of the martial arts. His notes eventually filled eight two-inch-thick notebooks. After his death these would be edited by Linda Lee and published as the volume *The Tao of Jeet Kune Do*, an outline of the philosophy and methods of "the way of intercepting fist."

Bruce was a great believer in the power of self-help and had long been a reader of the "positive thinkers" like Norman Vincent Peale and Napolean Hill. Consequently he refused to believe that he would be disabled for life, and was convinced instead that his will could triumph over the matter of his back. After six months he started exercising once again, and within a year seemed his old physical self. Away from the public gaze, however, he would suffer chronic pain for the rest of his short life.

Bruce decided to bring the same iron willpower to bear on his career. More than ever he was determined to be a major star and to introduce the world to kung fu, through the media of television and film. He began working frantically on an idea for a television show about a Shaolin monk who roamed the Old American West. Warner Bros. liked it and made it into the major hit series *Kung Fu*. To Bruce's intense disappointment, however, the starring role was given to David Carradine. The ABC-TV network considered Bruce too Asian-looking and too unknown a name to sustain a television series.

There was, though, one place in the world where Bruce Lee was neither too Chinese nor too insignificant a name. Early in 1971 he took a trip back to Hong Kong and found, to his surprise, that he was a veritable superstar there. *The Green Hornet*—retitled *The Kato Show*—was one of the most popular shows in Southeast Asia. The films he had made in childhood were screened over and over again. Bruce Lee was the proverbial local boy made good. A charismatic appearance on a Hong Kong television show, during which he cracked five dangling one-inch boards with a single kick, only served to confirm his idollike stature.

Bruce returned to Los Angeles, but almost as soon as he landed he received an offer from Raymond Chow, a Hong Kong film producer who had once worked for the Asian movie magnate Sir Run Run Shaw and had later set up his own Golden Harvest Studios. Chow offered to pay Bruce $15,000 for two Chinese martial arts features. Until then Bruce had thought of his future as being in Hollywood. But the money put up by Chow, plus his recent rapturous reception in Hong Kong, convinced him to return to the East.

In July 1971 Bruce arrived in the remote Thai village of Pak Chong for the shooting of his first film for Raymond Chow, *The Big Boss*. Meeting Chow for the first time, Bruce shook his hand and said, "I'm going to be the biggest Chinese star in the world." Chow looked him in the eye, saw the steely determination, and did not doubt him.

The Big Boss, *an on-set portrait*

Scene from The Big Boss

THE BIG BOSS

Pak Chong was a humid, cockroach-ridden hamlet with little to recommend it. Fresh vegetables and meat were scarce, and Bruce relied on bottle after bottle of vitamin pills to keep his body going during the six weeks of filming.

Trouble soon brewed on the set. Directors came and went until the cigar-smoking Lo Wei, Raymond Chow's senior cinematic helmsman, took over the show. There was no proper stunt equipment, and during the first week of shooting, Bruce fell on a slipped mattress and sprained his ankle. While convalescing from this accident he came down with the flu. He also badly missed Linda and his children, who were still in Los Angeles. Yet by the time of the final wrap, Bruce had high hopes for the film as a martial arts action movie, and was especially pleased with his own performance. The premiere was set for early October in Hong Kong.

In the meantime, Bruce was flown back to the States by the Hollywood studio Paramount. An episode of the crime show *Longstreet*, entitled "The Way of the Intercepting Fist" and guest-starring and cowritten by Bruce, had just aired in the United States to thundering acclaim. Paramount offered Bruce $3,000 for another three appearances. Bruce made the studio pay him $6,000, plus a technical advisor's fee.

(He was disappointed by the episodes; he had to be worked into existing storylines, which meant that his parts were only walk-ons.) There were others knocking at Bruce's door, too. Warner Bros.—which had dumped his film project *The Silent Flute* and had given the lead in *Kung Fu* to Carradine—wanted to place him under television option for $25,000. Run Run Shaw made weekly overtures to woo Bruce away from Raymond Chow, even sending him a blank check and telling him to fill it out for any amount he desired.

With his mind whirling with offers and counteroffers, Bruce flew to Hong Kong for the premiere of *The Big Boss*, accompanied by Linda, Brandon, and Shannon. They landed at the airport and were met by ranks of screaming fans and frantic reporters. Airport police had to escort the Lees out.

The premiere of *The Big Boss* took place at midnight on a balmy Hong Kong night. A huge billboard of Bruce Lee in fighting pose greeted the audience as they jostled to get a seat in the Movie Palace. For over two hours the audience watched Bruce, bare-chested, battle with legions of Thai adversaries, who all fell before his famous straight punch or a kick to the jaw. In one scene Bruce emitted his *kiai* (fighting yell) and mowed down fifteen opponents, who were made to look like amateurs. The ending was unusual by the rigid rules of Mandarin film drama, with the hero hauled off in chains. For a moment the theatre was morgue-silent, and then the audience went into a wild, standing applause. To the Chinese people of Hong Kong, Bruce Lee was more than a film star. He was the symbol of their identity and their aspirations, and filled their need for a real-life hero.

Bruce Lee was a man of loyalty. Despite the generous offers from others, he decided to fulfill the terms of his contract with Raymond Chow. The shooting of Bruce's next film for Chow, *Fist of Fury* (retitled *The Chinese Connection* in the United States and Britain), was in Hong Kong, and Golden Harvest installed the Lees at an apartment in the

They Died Too Young

Waterloo area of Kowloon. Brandon was enrolled at Bruce's alma mater, La Salle College, and Shannon was sent to a Chinese nursery school. Bruce himself worked long hours and was rarely home before three in the morning.

The filming of *Fist of Fury* was chaotic. There was no proper script and director Lo Wei seemed uninterested in the project. (He was once caught listening to a horse race on the radio when he was meant to be directing a love scene.) But the film's story was strong, and was guaranteed to please a Chinese audience. Set in 1908, it featured Bruce as a martial arts student whose *sifu* (teacher) dies. At the funeral, a delegation from a Japanese martial arts school insults the dead man by presenting a tablet inscribed to "The Sick Man of Asia." Bruce fights for the honor of his teacher, school, and race. As he beats the best that Japan can offer, Bruce roars, "The Chinese are not sick men!" In one cinematic stroke, all the humiliation that the Chinese felt from their occupation by Japan during the Second World War was expiated. Audiences loved it.

Fist of Fury smashed box-office records everywhere in Southeast Asia. Although critics noted that Lo Wei had mishandled the film, they praised Bruce's fighting techniques, which were more lethal than ever, and included his first screen use of *nunchaku* (Filipino double sticks). Also singled out was Bruce's acting ability, and his deft use of comedy to make fools of his enemies. He could act, and he could fight like no one else on earth. On screen, he gave off a violent, wild animal charisma.

Bruce Lee was now the hottest film property east of Hollywood.

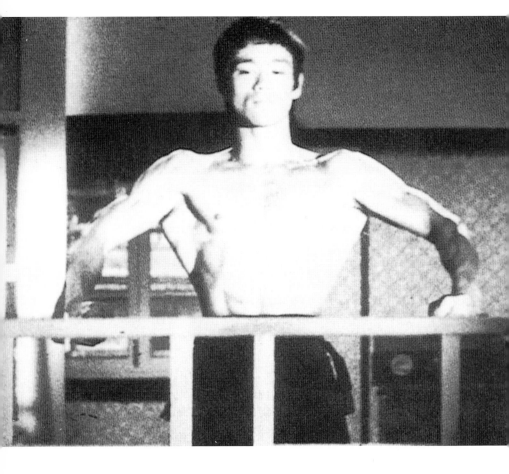

Muscles flexed, Way of the Dragon

THE WAYS OF THE DRAGON

With *Fist of Fury* completed, Bruce was a free agent. For a while he considered another Golden Harvest script, *The Yellow Faced Tiger*, but the appointed director—Lo Wei—refused Bruce's request that it should be rewritten by a professional screenwriter. Lo Wei, in the usual fashion of Chinese directors, wanted to use the script as a bare guide and make up the rest as he went along. Bruce bowed out of the project, and instead formed a joint production company, Concord, with Raymond Chow. Now, rather than being just the hired acting help, Lee was on equal footing with Chow. The problem of who would direct the next Bruce Lee film was easily solved: he would do it himself. For weeks he read and reread a library of books on filmmaking.

Bruce Lee was now actor, producer, and director, but he still needed the right script. Unable to find it, he decided that this too should be done by Bruce Lee. *The Way of the Dragon* (also known as *Return of the Dragon*) was solely a Bruce Lee project, the film by which he would advance simultaneously the frontiers of Mandarin and martial arts cinema. It became a total obsession.

The plot of *The Way of the Dragon* involved an innocent out-of-town boy, Tan Lung, trying to negotiate life in a busy foreign city (this became Rome, for the simple reason that

Raymond Chow had production contacts there). Like most of the heroes portrayed by Bruce, the yokel Tan Lung was slow to anger, but once roused was a two-legged killing machine, in this case of Chinese mobsters. There was a certain unexpected leaning toward comedy, but the real innovations in *The Way of the Dragon* were the use of Caucasians as bad guys (played by the imported U.S. karate champions Chuck Norris and Bob Wall), the specially arranged score, and the meticulously choreographed fight scenarios. For these Bruce videotaped countless wrestling and boxing matches—he was an ardent admirer of Muhammad Ali—and studied them frame by frame. The climactic big fight in *The Way of the Dragon,* between Bruce and Chuck Norris in the Colosseum, the ancient home of the gladiators, took twenty pages of written direction.

As might be expected from a directorial debut, the finished film had some roughness around the edges, but audiences in Hong Kong hardly cared. The picture grossed $5 million, more money than any film before it.

Now, for the first time in his life, Bruce Lee was wealthy. To celebrate he bought a Mercedes 350SL and moved the family into an elegant Kowloon town house. The days when he could not afford to repair his broken glasses were gone forever.

Bruce intended *The Way of the Dragon* to be the first of a trilogy featuring the Tan Lung character, but almost as soon as *Way* was in the can, he had an offer from Warner Bros. that was too good to refuse. At the bidding of a senior Warner Bros. producer, Fred Weintraub, the studio had agreed to put up $500,000 for the shooting of a martial arts movie provisionally entitled *Blood and Steel*, but which would eventually reach the cinema as *Enter the Dragon*. There was no doubt who would star in the movie. Fred Weintraub already knew Bruce from his time in Hollywood working on *The Green Hornet*, and was aware of his sensational impact on the cinema circuits of Asia.

They Died Too Young

In the Roman Colosseum, Rome, Way of the Dragon

By February 1973 Fred Weintraub, director Robert Clouse, and the costars of *Enter the Dragon*, John Saxon, Jim Kelly, and Ahna Capri, had arrived in Hong Kong, all to be met by Bruce and given his trademark greeting, a kick to the head which just skimmed the nose.

None of the shoots on Bruce's previous films had been easy, and *Enter the Dragon* proved no exception. Bruce was nervous about making his first international feature film, and delayed the start of work. There were innumerable problems of translation and cultural difference (not least that some of the American crew would not eat Chinese food). There were frequent injuries to the cast because of the lack of props and the realism of the action scenes. Bruce himself lacerated his hand on a broken glass bottle in a fight with Bob Wall. In another scene Bruce had to edge past a cobra, which bit him. Fortunately the serpent had been defanged, but it still caused an unpleasant wound.

The problems piled up. At one stage a strike was threatened by the martial arts extras when they discovered that Hong Kong prostitutes, hired to appear in a key scene, were paid at a higher rate than they were. Bruce himself threatened to quit after a clash with screenwriter Michael Allin, who had made the mistake of being disrespectful to Bruce. Fred Weintraub promised Bruce he would send Allin home to America, but in fact only moved him to another hotel in Hong Kong. This was a serious loss of face for Bruce. Only after days of rage and much peacemaking could he be persuaded to return to the set. There were also fiery, time-consuming disputes between Bruce and Raymond Chow, who was coproducing *Enter the Dragon*. Another problem was that the martial arts extras—most of whom were members of the Chinese crime syndicate, the Triads, would sometimes challenge Bruce to a real fight. For the most part Bruce would ignore it, but a few would persist and insult him, saying that he was frightened. To defend his honor, Bruce would then accept the challenge. He never lost.

A dramatic fling, Enter the Dragon

One person with whom Bruce did see eye to eye on the set was Robert Clouse, the director. Clouse thought that Lee's usual yokel character needed to be made more sophisticated—in a word, Westernized—for international consumption. Accordingly, he became Chen Chen, a Shaolin monk turned secret agent of impeccable taste and dress, whose mission was to bust a Hong Kong opium ring headed by the Fu Man Chu–like Han. Clouse also toned down Bruce's tendency to overdramatize in the classic fashion of Mandarin moviemaking. Bruce readily agreed to these changes.

For Bruce Lee, the future rode on the success or failure of *Enter the Dragon*. It was not every day that a Chinese actor was given star billing in a Hollywood movie. He worried and worked at every aspect of the film, a ball of nervous, creative energy. By the end of shooting he had lost weight and was existing on vitamin pills and herbal drinks. He was also finding that stardom exacted a heavy price. He could not move on the streets of Hong Kong without being mobbed. Newspapers pried into every aspect of his life. His personality changed. He became suspicious of people, less friendly, and a darkness settled around him. Only Linda received his complete trust.

Beginning on the afternoon of May 10, 1973, Bruce's body showed signs of breakdown. He was dubbing the sound to the final print of *Enter the Dragon* at the Golden Harvest studios, a former textile mill. He was already exhausted. The room was small, hot, and without air conditioning. He made a visit to the rest room, returned—and collapsed in a fit of vomiting and convulsions.

He was rushed to hospital. Linda was summoned and told he was "very sick." The convulsions got worse. Dr. Peter Woo, a leading neurosurgeon, was called in. He surmised that something was wrong with Bruce's brain, although he was not sure exactly what. The film star seemed near death. Woo administered the drug Manitol to reduce a swelling in Bruce's brain, and prepared for surgery in case this did not

They Died Too Young

work. Fortunately it did. Lee began to regain consciousness almost immediately. He could see and make signs of recognition, but he could not talk. It took several days for his speech to return.

A week later Bruce was flown to Los Angeles for a complete brain and body examination. No abnormalities were found. Concerning the collapse on May 10, it was suggested that Bruce had suffered cerebral edema (an excess of fluid surrounding the brain), though its cause could not be discerned. Bruce was prescribed Dilantin, a drug that calms brain activity.

The collapse left Bruce shaken, but it did nothing to diminish his work rate. There was no letup. Indeed, he worked harder. It was almost as if Bruce realized that he was in a race against time.

Three in battle, Enter the Dragon

THE GAME OF DEATH

The premiere of *Enter the Dragon* was set for August 10, 1973, in Hong Kong. Bruce spent the intervening time developing another movie there, *The Game of Death*. Some of the action scenes for this, in which Bruce fought the towering Kareem Abdul-Jabbar, had already been shot. (The film would be completed by Robert Clouse after Bruce's death with—ridiculously—an actor sporting a mask filling in for the kung fu star.) Bruce also made plans to move back to the United States with his family. And yet he knew that it would never happen. One day, suddenly, he turned to Linda and said, "I don't know how long I can keep this up."

The question was answered on July 20, 1973. Bruce spent the afternoon at his Kowloon house discussing the script of *The Game of Death* with Raymond Chow. Afterward they drove over to the home of Taiwanese actress Betty Ting-pei, who was to have the major female role in the film. Raymond went home to dress for a dinner he was having that night with Bruce and James Bond actor George Lazenby. They hoped to persuade Lazenby to costar alongside Bruce in the new feature.

Bruce, meanwhile, still at Betty Ting-pei's flat, had developed a headache. Betty gave him a tablet of Equagesic, a strong aspirin-based drug prescribed for her by her

Fast action, Game of Death

doctor. At around 7:30 P.M. Bruce went to lie down in a bedroom. He was still asleep at just after 9 P.M. when Raymond Chow telephoned to find out why he had not turned up at the restaurant. Betty said she could not wake Bruce. Raymond went over to Betty's apartment, where he found Bruce in an extremely deep sleep. They called a doctor, who arrived almost immediately and spent ten minutes trying to revive the kung fu star.

At ten o'clock an ambulance sped Bruce to the Queen Elizabeth Hospital. Raymond telephoned Linda and told her to go there right away. When Bruce arrived at the hospital, doctors rushed him into an intensive care unit and began massaging his heart. This was quickly followed by the injection of stimulatory drugs directly into the heart and electric shocks. It was no use. Bruce Lee was already dead. He was just thirty-two.

There were two funeral ceremonies. The first was in Hong Kong, where there was a traditional Buddhist service. Outside the Kowloon Funeral Parlour, a crowd of twenty-five thousand fans wept and wailed. The second, more private ceremony was in Seattle, where Bruce and Linda had met and where Bruce had perhaps been at his happiest. The pallbearers were led by James Coburn and Steve McQueen. Bruce was buried in the city's Lake View Cemetery, dressed in the Chinese outfit he had worn in *Enter the Dragon*. The final eulogy was spoken by James Coburn, "Farewell, brother. It has been an honor to share this space in time with you. As a friend and as a teacher, you have given to me, have brought my physical, spiritual, and psychological selves together. Thank you." The tombstone was inscribed simply, "Bruce Lee. Nov. 27, 1940–July 20, 1973. Founder of Jeet Kune Do."

Almost inevitably, the death of Bruce Lee was followed by wild speculation, as it is with all stars who die before they get old. Some believed that Bruce was still alive. Others thought that he had been murdered, either by the Triads

Right foot forward, Game of Death

or by jealous film rivals. There was a lengthy coroner's inquest in Hong Kong. A panel of medical experts concluded that he died from a hypersensitive reaction to a compound in the drug Equagesic. The hypersensitivity led to edema, a swelling of the brain, and caused Bruce to enter a sleep from which he never awoke. The coroner announced that he was satisfied with the finding of the physicians. So did Linda Lee.

Only days after Bruce's burial, *Enter the Dragon* received its premiere at Grauman's Chinese Theatre in Hollywood. The film was an instant hit in the States, and soon took the rest of the world by storm. The worldwide theatrical gross is currently over $200,000,000. Since the complete cost of making the film was $800,000, this makes *Enter the Dragon* one of the most profitable pictures of all time. It also made Bruce a mythical cult figure, whose star shines brighter with every passing year. He paved the way for many other martial arts actors—Jackie Chan, Chuck Norris, Jean Claude Van Damme—but he was more than a trailblazer. He was the original and the best. Wherever people gather to watch action movies, they will screen the films of The Dragon.

A subdued scene, The Big Boss

POSTSCRIPT

Twenty years later the tragedy of early death was to afflict the Lee family once again. On March 31, 1993, Bruce's charismatic son, Brandon, who had followed in his father's footsteps as a film star, died during the shooting of an action sequence in *The Crow*. He was only twenty-nine.

Bruce Lee in Hong Kong for filming

FILMOGRAPHY

The year refers to the first release date of the film.

1966–67	*The Green Hornet* (television series)
1972	*The Big Boss*
1972	*Fist of Fury* (*The Chinese Connection*)
1973	*The Way of the Dragon* (*Return of the Dragon*)
1973	*Enter the Dragon*
1974	*Game of Death*

On the attack, Fists of Fury

INDEX

INDEX

Enter the Dragon, *away from combat*